MUSICAL INSTRUMENTS OF THE WORLD

Woodwind and Brass

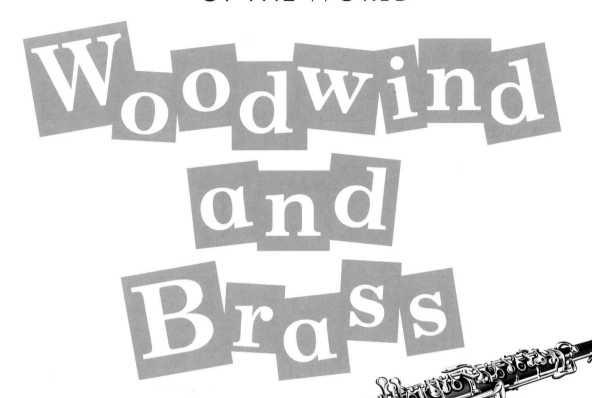

Barrie Carson Turner

Illustrated by John See

Smart Apple Media

First published in the UK in 1998 by
Belitha Press Limited
London House, Great Eastern Wharf,
Parkgate Road, London SW11 4NQ

Text by Barrie Carson Turner   Illustrations by John See
Text and illustrations copyright © Belitha Press Ltd 1998
Cover design by The Design Lab

Published in the United States by
Smart Apple Media
123 South Broad Street
Mankato, Minnesota 56001

ISBN: 1-887068-48-1

Library of Congress Cataloging-in-Publication Data

Turner, Barrie.
    Woodwinds and brass / Barrie Carson Turner.
        p.   cm. — (The musical instruments of the world)
    Includes index.
    Summary: Describes nineteen wind instruments from around the world
including the oboe, didjeridu, bassoon, and accordion.
    ISBN 1-887068-48-1
    1. Wind instruments—Juvenile literature.   [1. Wind instruments.]
I. Title. II. Series.
ML930.T88 1998
788'. 19—dc21   98-6281

Printed in Hong Kong / China

9 8 7 6 5 4 3 2 1

Picture acknowledgements Eye Ubiquitous: 10, 15 David Cumming;
Robert Harding Picture Library: 6 A. Woolfitt, 20-21 Rolf Richardson,
28-29 Ken Gilham; The Hutchison Library: 4-5 Trevor Page, 22 P. Moszynski;
Panos Pictures: 9; Performing Arts Library: 11-12 James McCormick,
16-17 Clive Barda; Redferns: 19, 26 Odile Noel, 23 Henrietta Butler,
24-25 David Redfern; Royal Scottish National Orchestra: 14 Stephen West;
Stock Market: 7, 27; Trip: 18 V. Sidoropolev; John Walmsley Photo Library: 8, 13.

Contents

Musical

Musical instruments are played in every country of the world. There are many thousands of instruments in all shapes and sizes. They are often grouped into four families: strings, brass, percussion, and woodwind.

Brass and woodwind instruments are blown to make their sound. Stringed instruments sound when their strings vibrate. Percussion instruments are struck (hit), shaken, or scraped to make their sound.

instruments

For this book we have chosen 19 brass and woodwind instruments. Brass players press their lips tightly together and blow air through them to make their instruments sound. Woodwind instruments are made to sound in different ways. The woodwinds in this book all have a reed that vibrates when air is blown into the mouthpiece.

There is a picture of each instrument and a photograph of a performer playing it. On pages 30 and 31 you will find a list of useful words to help you understand more about music.

B
W

On each page you will see a **B** or a **W** in a colored box. **B** means the instrument is from the brass family. **W** means the instrument is from the woodwind family.

Oboe

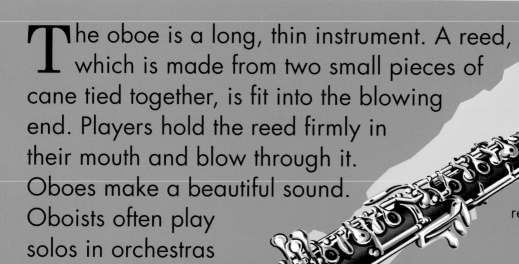

The oboe is a long, thin instrument. A reed, which is made from two small pieces of cane tied together, is fit into the blowing end. Players hold the reed firmly in their mouth and blow through it. Oboes make a beautiful sound. Oboists often play solos in orchestras and ensembles.

reed

finger hole

key

Oboes have finger holes and keys. Oboe players (oboists) cover and uncover the holes and press the keys to make different notes.

Trumpet

The trumpet is a well-known brass instrument. Its sound is exciting and loud. Trumpets are made from a long, tightly-coiled metal tube. One end has a mouthpiece. At the other end the tube opens out into a cone called the bell.

B

bell

mouthpiece

valve

Players press down three small buttons, called valves, to make different notes. Trumpet players are called trumpeters. They play in orchestras, jazz bands, and marching bands.

7

Clarinet

mouthpiece

The clarinet has a wide range of notes, from low to high. The player covers the finger holes and presses metal keys to make different notes. A thin, flat piece of cane, called a reed, is fixed to the mouthpiece. When the clarinet player (clarinettist) blows into the mouthpiece, the reed vibrates and the instrument makes sounds.

W

finger hole

key

The clarinet can be heard in many different kinds of music, including orchestras, small ensembles, and jazz groups.

Cornet

The cornet is made from a coiled metal tube. It is shorter than the trumpet, and its sound is not as bright. It has three buttons called valves. When the player presses them, the valves open and close parts of the tube, making different notes.

valve

bell

mouthpiece

B

The cornet is usually played in brass bands. It often plays solo.

9

Conch

The conch is made from the shell of a large shellfish. The end of the shell is cut off or a hole is made in the side, and the instrument is blown like a trumpet. The conch has been used to call workers from the fields or to call soldiers to war. The conch is is still played at some religious festivals.

blow hole

The conch makes a loud sound that can be heard from far away. A conch is sometimes called a shell trumpet. But unlike a trumpet, a conch can only sound one note.

B

Bassoon

crook

reed

The bassoon is a very large woodwind instrument. The finger holes are covered by small metal caps called keys. Near the top there is a curved metal tube called a crook. The crook makes it easier for players to reach the mouthpiece and the keys at the same time. Players wear a neck strap to help hold the instrument.

Bassoon players (bassoonists) make a sound by blowing into a reed. The bassoon sounds like an oboe, but its notes are much lower.

key

11

French horn

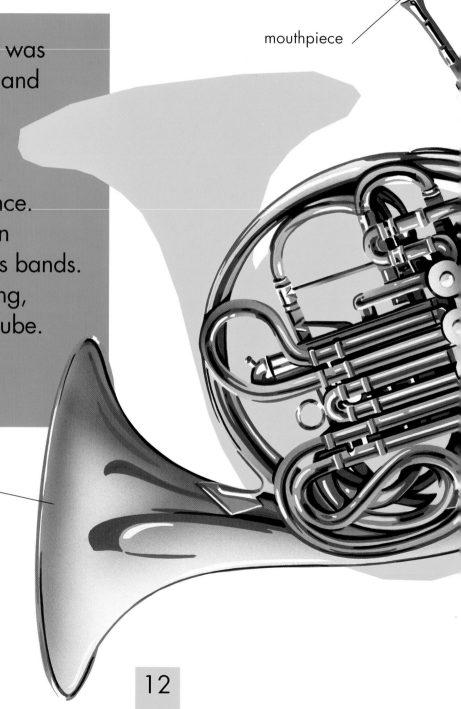

mouthpiece

The French horn was brought to England from France 300 years ago and has been called the French horn ever since. It is usually played in orchestras and brass bands. It is made from a long, coiled, shiny metal tube. If uncoiled, it would stretch several feet.

B

bell

Players press three small levers called valves to make many different notes. Musicians also press their lips tightly into the mouthpiece. Players can make different notes by changing the shape of their lips. Notes can sound low and warm or high and bright.

valve

French horn players place their right hand in the bell as they play. This position helps to hold the horn and improve its sound.

Cor anglais

reed

crook

W

Cor anglais (cor-on-glay) means English horn. It looks like a big oboe. Players blow through a reed, which fits into a long metal tube at the top. The bottom end is shaped like a pear and is called the bell. Most of the finger holes are covered by small metal caps called keys.

key

bell

The cor anglais sounds lower than the oboe, but higher than a bassoon. The instrument has a rich, dreamy sound.

14

Pungi

gourd

The pungi (pun-ji) comes from India. This instrument has two pipes at the bottom. One pipe sounds only one note. The player covers and uncovers the finger holes on the other pipe to make more notes. The round body is made from a gourd (a pear-shaped fruit).

W

finger hole

Players blow into one end of the gourd. They need a lot of breath to make the pungi's unusual whining sound.

Sousaphone

The sousaphone (sooz-a-fone) was named about 100 years ago, after American composer John Philip Sousa. Sousa wanted a new brass instrument that could play very low notes, so he decided to invent one.

B

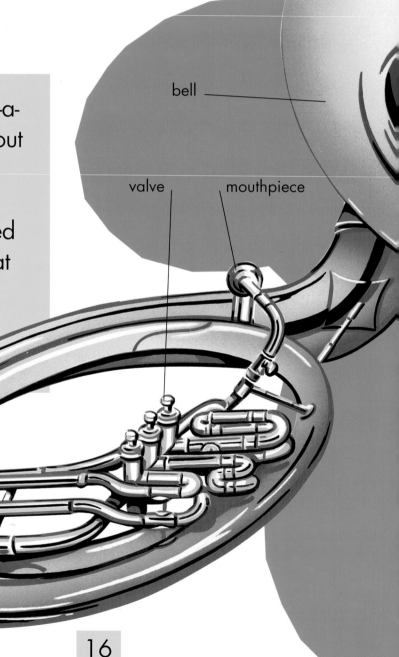

bell

valve   mouthpiece

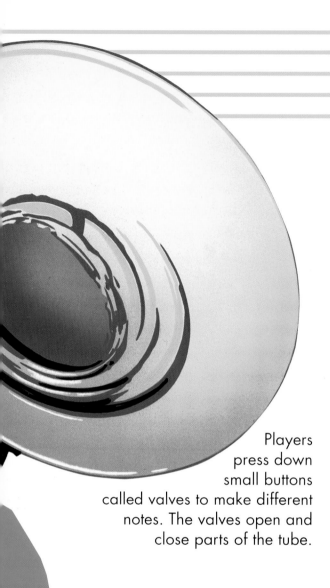

Players press down small buttons called valves to make different notes. The valves open and close parts of the tube.

The sousaphone is so big that it has to be looped around the player's body and rest on the left shoulder. Its huge bell faces toward the audience. Brass sousaphones are very heavy. Modern ones are often made from fiberglass, which is much lighter.

Zurna

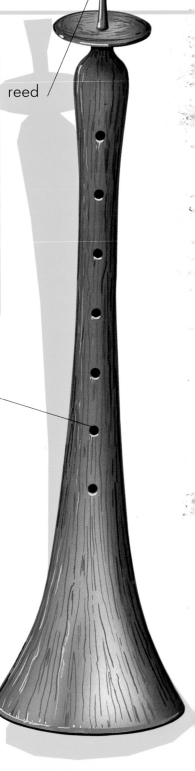

reed

The zurna comes from Turkey. This instrument is carved from wood and is often decorated with silver. Like the oboe, the zurna has two small pieces of cane that fit into the blowing end. They are shaped like a tiny fan and are tied tightly together. This is called the reed.

The zurna is often played at weddings and festivals. The player holds the reed tightly in the mouth and blows through the reed to make a strong, buzzing sound.

finger hole

W

Trombone

The trombone is made from a long metal tube that is coiled around twice. The tube opens at the far end into a trumpet shape. Part of the tubing is called the slide. The player moves the slide in and out to make different notes. Trombone players are called trombonists. They have to blow hard to make a sound.

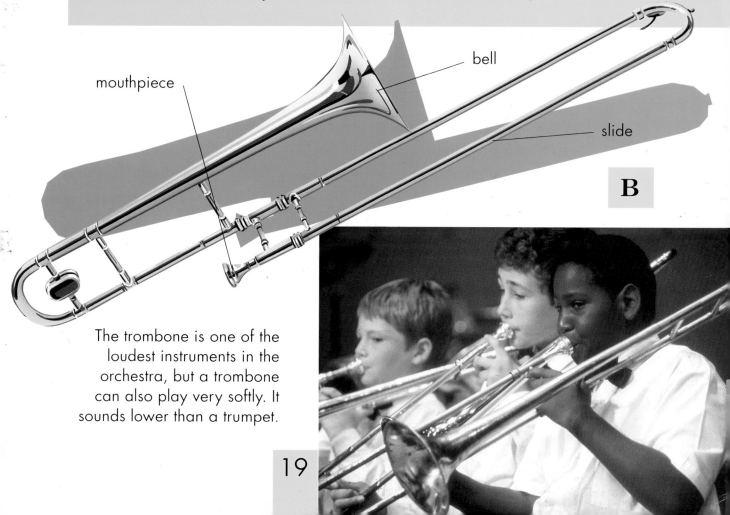

bell

mouthpiece

slide

B

The trombone is one of the loudest instruments in the orchestra, but a trombone can also play very softly. It sounds lower than a trumpet.

Saxophone

The saxophone is a woodwind instrument that is made of metal! The instrument was invented about 150 years ago by a Belgian instrument maker, Adolphe Sax. Like the clarinet, it has a flat piece of cane called a reed fixed to the mouthpiece with a thin band of metal. When the saxophone player blows into the mouthpiece, the reed vibrates and the instrument sounds.

mouthpiece

The finger holes on a saxophone are covered by small metal keys. The player presses on the keys, which open and close the holes to make different notes.

W

key

bell

Saxophones are made in seven different sizes. The highest-pitched is called a sopranino. The lowest-pitched, called a contrabass, is about 6 1/2 feet (2.6 m) long. Saxophones are usually played in jazz and rock music. They make a rich, smooth sound.

Sheng

The sheng is a mouth organ. It was first played in China thousands of years ago. At the bottom of each pipe there is a thin piece of metal called a reed. When air passes through the pipes, the reed vibrates and the instrument sounds. Each pipe plays a different note.

pipe

Players make the sheng sound by blowing and sucking on the mouthpiece.

W

finger hole

mouthpiece

22

Euphonium

The euphonium (u-fo-ni-um) is like a small tuba. It is made from a long metal tube coiled many times. At the end, the tube widens into a large cone shape called the bell. Players press down four small buttons, called valves, to make different notes.

bell

mouthpiece

B

valve

The euphonium is usually played in brass bands. You can often hear it playing a solo. Its sound is warm and mellow.

Accordion

The accordion is an unusual woodwind instrument. On one side it has a small piano keyboard. On the other side there are many finger buttons. In the middle there are bellows. Musicians play the tune on the keyboard. They press the buttons to play the accompaniment.

keyboard

W

The accordion often plays dance and folk music. The instrument hangs around the player's neck by a strap. An accordion makes a wheezy sound.

24

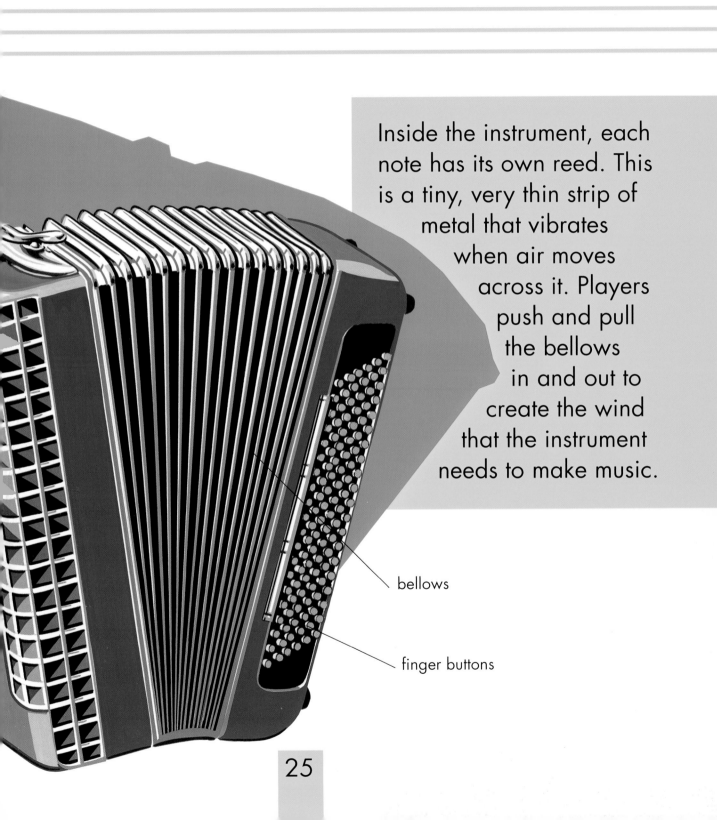

Inside the instrument, each note has its own reed. This is a tiny, very thin strip of metal that vibrates when air moves across it. Players push and pull the bellows in and out to create the wind that the instrument needs to make music.

bellows

finger buttons

Didjeridu

blowing
end

The didjeridu (di-jerr-i-doo) comes from Australia. This instrument is made from a long, hollow tree branch. Players need a lot of breath to play the didjeridu. They press their lips tightly into the hollow tube and blow through it to make a sound. It is important that no air escapes as they blow.

A didjeridu usually has only one note, but players use their mouth, lips, and voice to make the note sound in different ways.

hollow tube

B

Tuba

The tuba is the biggest and lowest-sounding brass instrument in an orchestra. Players press their lips tightly into the mouthpiece and blow to make a sound. They can make different notes by changing the shape of their lips as they blow. Because the tuba is so big, it takes a lot of breath to play.

bell

valve

mouthpiece

B

The tuba is played in orchestras and brass bands. Musicians play sitting down, with the tuba resting on their knees.

27

Bagpipes

Bagpipe players fill the instrument's bag with air by blowing into the blowpipe. The bag must be kept full of air all the time. Once it is full, the air can only escape through the pipes. Each pipe has a reed. When the bag is squeezed by the player's arm, the air is forced into the pipes and creates a sound.

drone pipe

Bagpipes are played in many parts of the world. In Scotland they are played at important events. They have a shrill wailing sound and can be heard from far away.

W

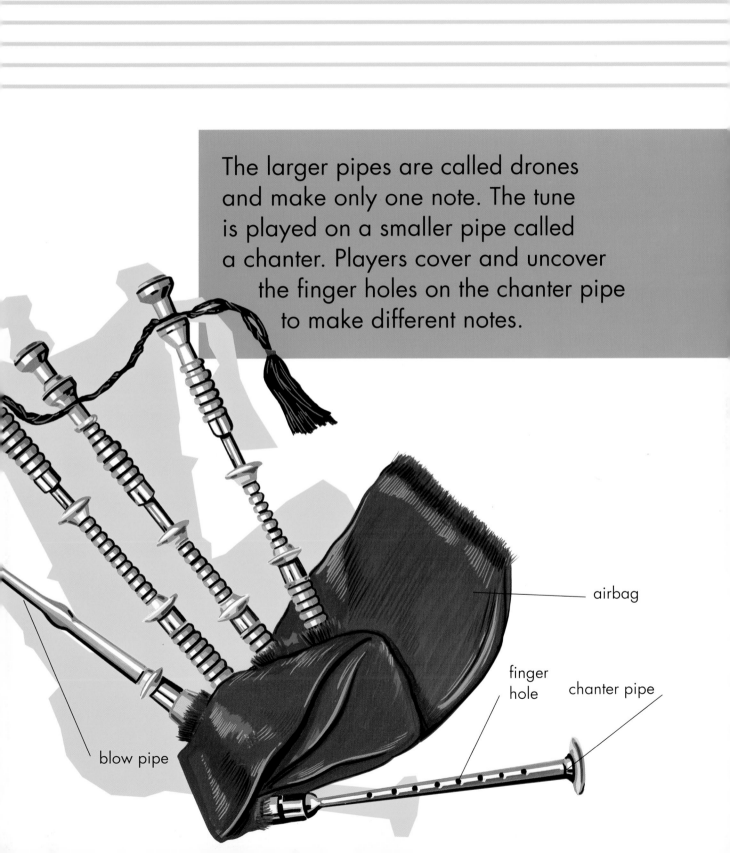

The larger pipes are called drones and make only one note. The tune is played on a smaller pipe called a chanter. Players cover and uncover the finger holes on the chanter pipe to make different notes.

airbag

finger hole

chanter pipe

blow pipe

Words to

accompaniment Notes that are played along with the tune.

audience People who listen to musicians playing or singing.

bell The wide end of a brass or woodwind instrument.

bellows The part of an instrument that holds air. When a player squeezes the bellows, the instrument makes a sound.

brass band An orchestra of brass instruments.

composer A person who composes (writes) music.

crook An extra piece of tubing on some long instruments that helps players reach all of the finger holes.

ensemble A small group of musicians playing together.

family (of instruments) Instruments that are similar to each other.

festival A special event, often with music and dancing.

fiberglass A material made of glass. It is lighter than metal.

finger holes The holes a player covers to make different notes.

folk music Popular songs or tunes that are so old that no one knows who wrote them.

jazz A kind of pop music. In jazz, musicians often make up the music as they play.

keyboard Notes, called keys, laid out as they are on a piano.

key (on a woodwind instrument) A small metal cap covering a finger hole.

remember

marching band A group of musicians who play military (soldiers') music as they march along.

mellow A word used to describe a soft, warm, gentle sound.

mouth organ An instrument blown by the mouth. It sounds like an organ.

mouthpiece The part of a wind or brass instrument that is held in the mouth and blown.

musician Someone who plays an instrument or sings.

orchestra A large group of musicians playing together.

performer Someone who plays or sings to other people.

reed A tiny, thin piece of metal or cane that vibrates and makes the sound in some wind instruments.

rock A type of pop music that often has a strong beat.

solo A piece of music played or sung by one performer.

valves Small buttons or levers that a brass instrument player presses to make different notes.

vibrate To move up and down very quickly, like shaking. When air passes over a reed, it vibrates.

wind band An orchestra of woodwind instruments.

Index